ON THE WATER

Surfing

by Rachel Grack

BLASTOFF! READERS 2

BLASTOFF! READERS, AN IMPRINT OF BELLWETHER MEDIA BY FLUTTERBEE

Blastoff! Readers are carefully developed by literacy experts to build reading stamina and move students toward fluency by combining standards-based content with developmentally appropriate text.

Level 1 provides the most support through repetition of high-frequency words, light text, predictable sentence patterns, and strong visual support.

Level 2 offers early readers a bit more challenge through varied sentences, increased text load, and text-supportive special features.

Level 3 advances early-fluent readers toward fluency through increased text load, less reliance on photos, advancing concepts, longer sentences, and more complex special features.

★ **Blastoff! Universe**

This edition first published in 2027 by Bellwether Media, Inc.

For information regarding permission, write to Bellwether Media, Inc., Attention: Permissions Department, 3500 American Blvd W, Suite 150, Bloomington, MN 55431.

Library of Congress Cataloging-in-Publication Data is available at www.loc.gov or upon request from the publisher.

ISBN: 9798898800604 (hardcover)
ISBN: 9798898801847 (ebook)

Editor: Kieran Downs   Series Designer: Josh Brink   Designer: Laura Sowers

Printed in the United States of America, North Mankato, MN.

Table of Contents

Ride the Waves

Surfing is the sport of riding boards on **breaking** waves.

People surf on ocean waves. Some lakes and rivers have **surf breaks** as well.

Top Place to Surf

North Shore, Hawai'i, United States

Free surfers ride the waves for fun. They create their own styles.

Some surfers **compete** to show off their surfing skills.

There are many types of surfboards. Longboards made of foam are best for beginners. They are wide and **stable**.

Skilled surfers often use shortboards.

longboard
shortboard

Surfers wear swimsuits.
They may wear wetsuits
in cold water.

Surf wax makes boards less slippery. **Leashes** connect boards to surfers.

What Surfers Need

Getting Started on Surfing

surfing lesson

Many people take surfing lessons. They learn skills on land first.

Beginners surf in **shallow** waters with sandy bottoms. They practice on small waves.

shallow water

Surfers walk into the water. Once the water meets their waists, they lie on their boards on their stomachs.

They wait in the **lineup** for their turn.

paddling

Surfers paddle out toward the waves. Then they turn to face the shore. They wait for a wave.

Surfers paddle with the speed of the wave as it comes near.

Surfers pop up to their feet when they catch a wave.

How to Surf

They stand sideways on their boards. They **balance** while they ride.

Surf's Up!

Surfers ride in safe spots.
They watch the weather.

They respect other surfers. They give space and take turns. Surf's up!

Glossary

balance—to stay upright

breaking—curling over and falling apart

compete—to try to win something that someone else is also trying to win

leashes—ropes that connect surfboards to surfers

lineup—the area where surfers wait for a wave

shallow—not deep

stable—not likely to tip over

surf breaks—areas where waves break in ways surfers can ride them

To Learn More

AT THE LIBRARY

Mazzarella, Kerri. *Longboard Surfing.* New York, N.Y.: Crabtree Publishing, 2025.

Morey, Allan. *Surfing.* Mankato, Minn.: Black Rabbit Books, 2024.

Vonder Brink, Tracy. *Surfing.* Minneapolis, Minn.: Jump!, 2025.

ON THE WEB

FACTSURFER

Factsurfer.com gives you a safe, fun way to find more information.

1. Go to www.factsurfer.com.
2. Enter "surfing" into the search box and click 🔍.
3. Select your book cover to see a list of related content.

Index

The images in this book are reproduced through the courtesy of: Jandrie Lombard, front cover (top); SerrNovik, front cover (bottom); truphotovideo, p. 3; Denis Moskvinov, p. 4; ohrim, pp. 4-5; Ritu Manoj Jethani, p. 5; EpicStockMedia, pp. 6-7; Gaellh, p. 7; Sergey Novikov, pp. 8, 11; Daria Kulkova, pp. 8-9; Kirk Wester, pp. 10-11; Candy Retriever, p. 11 (wax); GM, pp. 12-13; pavlovski, p. 13; Vera Larina, pp. 14-15; Everlight Visuals, p. 15; Dudarev Mikhail, p. 16; SOMA surf-therapy, pp. 16-17; Tropical studio, pp. 18-19, 20-21; Nilanka Sampath, p. 19 (paddle, position, pop-up, carve); Kelly Headrick, p. 21; Sura Nualpradid, p. 23.